THE PEARSON

Student Planner

Academic Year
_____

Personal Information

Name: _____

Address: _____

Phone Number: _____

Email: _____

College Web site: _____

Emergency Contact: _____

PEARSON

New York   Boston   San Francisco
London   Toronto   Sydney   Tokyo   Singapore   Madrid
Mexico City   Munich   Paris   Cape Town   Hong Kong   Montreal

Senior Acquisitions Editors: Kate Edwards and Matt Wright
Editorial Assistants: Lindsey Allen and Haley Pero
Senior Supplements Editor: Donna Campion
Page layout: Teresa Ward

The Pearson Student Planner

ISBN-10: 0-205-66301-X

ISBN-13: 978-0-205-66301-9

1 2 3 4 5 6 7 8 9 10–CW–11 10 09 08

Important Information

Academic Advisor	Phone:	Email:
	Office:	Hours:
Library Hours		
Writing Center		
Financial Aid Office		
Career Center		
Student Health Center		
Registration Date		
Class Start Date		
Class End Date		

Schedule For

Time	Monday	Tuesday	Wednesday	Thursday	Friday	Saturday/Sunday
8:00 A.M.						
8:30						
9:00						
9:30						
10:00						
10:30						
11:00						
11:30						
12:00						
12:30						
1:00						
1:30						
2:00						
2:30						
3:00						
3:30						
4:00						
4:30						
5:00						
5:30						
6:00						
6:30						
7:00						
7:30						
8:00						
8:30						
9:00 P.M.						

Subject / Instructor / Office Hours / Telephone / Location

Subject / Instructor / Office Hours / Telephone / Location

Subject / Instructor / Office Hours / Telephone / Location

Subject / Instructor / Office Hours / Telephone / Location

Subject / Instructor / Office Hours / Telephone / Location

Schedule For

Time	Monday	Tuesday	Wednesday	Thursday	Friday	Saturday/Sunday
8:00 A.M.						
8:30						
9:00						
9:30						
10:00						
10:30						
11:00						
11:30						
12:00						
12:30						
1:00						
1:30						
2:00						
2:30						
3:00						
3:30						
4:00						
4:30						
5:00						
5:30						
6:00						
6:30						
7:00						
7:30						
8:00						
8:30						
9:00 P.M.						

Subject
Instructor
Office Hours
Telephone
Location

Subject
Instructor
Office Hours
Telephone
Location

Subject
Instructor
Office Hours
Telephone
Location

Subject
Instructor
Office Hours
Telephone
Location

Subject
Instructor
Office Hours
Telephone
Location

Schedule For

Time	Monday	Tuesday	Wednesday	Thursday	Friday	Saturday/Sunday
8:00 A.M.						
8:30						
9:00						
9:30						
10:00						
10:30						
11:00						
11:30						
12:00						
12:30						
1:00						
1:30						
2:00						
2:30						
3:00						
3:30						
4:00						
4:30						
5:00						
5:30						
6:00						
6:30						
7:00						
7:30						
8:00						
8:30						
9:00 P.M.						

Subject
Instructor
Office Hours
Telephone
Location

Subject
Instructor
Office Hours
Telephone
Location

Subject
Instructor
Office Hours
Telephone
Location

Subject
Instructor
Office Hours
Telephone
Location

Subject
Instructor
Office Hours
Telephone
Location

Schedule For

Time	Monday	Tuesday	Wednesday	Thursday	Friday	Saturday/Sunday
8:00 A.M.						
8:30						
9:00						
9:30						
10:00						
10:30						
11:00						
11:30						
12:00						
12:30						
1:00						
1:30						
2:00						
2:30						
3:00						
3:30						
4:00						
4:30						
5:00						
5:30						
6:00						
6:30						
7:00						
7:30						
8:00						
8:30						
9:00 P.M.						

Subject / Instructor / Office Hours / Telephone / Location

Subject / Instructor / Office Hours / Telephone / Location

Subject / Instructor / Office Hours / Telephone / Location

Subject / Instructor / Office Hours / Telephone / Location

Subject / Instructor / Office Hours / Telephone / Location

Schedule For

Subject
Instructor
Office Hours
Telephone
Location

Subject
Instructor
Office Hours
Telephone
Location

Subject
Instructor
Office Hours
Telephone
Location

Subject
Instructor
Office Hours
Telephone
Location

Subject
Instructor
Office Hours
Telephone
Location

Time	Monday	Tuesday	Wednesday	Thursday	Friday	Saturday/Sunday
8:00 A.M.						
8:30						
9:00						
9:30						
10:00						
10:30						
11:00						
11:30						
12:00						
12:30						
1:00						
1:30						
2:00						
2:30						
3:00						
3:30						
4:00						
4:30						
5:00						
5:30						
6:00						
6:30						
7:00						
7:30						
8:00						
8:30						
9:00 P.M.						

Schedule For

Time	Monday	Tuesday	Wednesday	Thursday	Friday	Saturday/ Sunday
8:00 A.M.						
8:30						
9:00						
9:30						
10:00						
10:30						
11:00						
11:30						
12:00						
12:30						
1:00						
1:30						
2:00						
2:30						
3:00						
3:30						
4:00						
4:30						
5:00						
5:30						
6:00						
6:30						
7:00						
7:30						
8:00						
8:30						
9:00 P.M.						

Subject / Instructor / Office Hours / Telephone / Location

Subject / Instructor / Office Hours / Telephone / Location

Subject / Instructor / Office Hours / Telephone / Location

Subject / Instructor / Office Hours / Telephone / Location

Subject / Instructor / Office Hours / Telephone / Location

Event Calendar

Record birthdays, anniversaries, and other special occasions.

January

- National Volunteer Blood Donor Month
- National Poverty in America Awareness Month
- National Book Month

February

- Black History Month
- Youth Leadership Month
- American Heart Month

March

- National Women's History Month
- Irish American Heritage Month
- Anonymous Giving Month

April

- National Poetry Month
- Alcohol Awareness Month
- National Teaching and Joy Month

May

- National Physical Fitness and Sports Month
- Asian Pacific American Heritage Month
- Better Sleep Month

June

- Adopt-A-Cat Month
- National Fresh Fruit and Vegetable Month
- Recycling Month

July

- National Recreation and Parks Month
- National Purposeful Parenting Month
- Cell Phone Courtesy Month

August

- National Water Quality Month
- National Immunization Awareness Month
- International Air Travel Month

September

- Hispanic Heritage Month (9/15–10/15)
- Library Card Sign-Up Month
- National School Success Month

October

- National Breast Cancer Awareness Month
- Banned Books Month
- National Cookie Month

November

- National American Indian Heritage Month
- Family Stories Month
- National AIDS Awareness Month

December

- National Stress-Free Family Holidays Month
- National Closed Caption TV Month
- Universal Human Rights Month

Month At-A-Glance

Month_____

Sunday	Monday	Tuesday	Wednesday	Thursday	Friday	Saturday

Month At-A-Glance

Month_____

Sunday	Monday	Tuesday	Wednesday	Thursday	Friday	Saturday

Month At-A-Glance

Month_____

Sunday	Monday	Tuesday	Wednesday	Thursday	Friday	Saturday

Month At-A-Glance

Month_____

Sunday	Monday	Tuesday	Wednesday	Thursday	Friday	Saturday

Month At-A-Glance

Month_____

Sunday	Monday	Tuesday	Wednesday	Thursday	Friday	Saturday

Month At-A-Glance

Month_____

Sunday	Monday	Tuesday	Wednesday	Thursday	Friday	Saturday

Month At-A-Glance

Month_____

Sunday	Monday	Tuesday	Wednesday	Thursday	Friday	Saturday

Month At-A-Glance

Month_____

Sunday	Monday	Tuesday	Wednesday	Thursday	Friday	Saturday

Month At-A-Glance

Month_____

Sunday	Monday	Tuesday	Wednesday	Thursday	Friday	Saturday

Month At-A-Glance

Month_____

Sunday	Monday	Tuesday	Wednesday	Thursday	Friday	Saturday

Month At-A-Glance

Month_____

Sunday	Monday	Tuesday	Wednesday	Thursday	Friday	Saturday

Month At-A-Glance

Month_____

Sunday	Monday	Tuesday	Wednesday	Thursday	Friday	Saturday

Month At-A-Glance

Month_____

Sunday	Monday	Tuesday	Wednesday	Thursday	Friday	Saturday

Month At-A-Glance

Month_____

Sunday	Monday	Tuesday	Wednesday	Thursday	Friday	Saturday

Weekly Schedule

Month: _____   **Reminders/Assignments**

Monday	

Tuesday	

Wednesday	

Notes/To Do

Thursday		

Friday		

Saturday		Sunday	

Weekly Schedule

Month: _____   **Reminders/Assignments**

Monday	

Tuesday	

Wednesday	

Notes/To Do	

Thursday	

Friday	

Saturday		Sunday	

Weekly Schedule

Month: _____   **Reminders/Assignments**

Monday	

Tuesday	

Wednesday	

Notes/To Do	

Thursday	

Friday	

Saturday	Sunday

Weekly Schedule

Month: _____

Reminders/Assignments

Monday	

Tuesday	

Wednesday	

Notes/To Do	

Thursday			

Friday			

Saturday		Sunday	

Weekly Schedule

Month: _____   **Reminders/Assignments**

Monday	

Tuesday	

Wednesday	

Notes/To Do

Thursday	
Friday	
Saturday		Sunday	

Weekly Schedule

Month: _____   **Reminders/Assignments**

Monday	

Tuesday	

Wednesday	

Notes/To Do

Thursday	

Friday	

Saturday		Sunday	

Weekly Schedule

Month: _____

Monday	

Tuesday	

Wednesday	

Notes/To Do	

Thursday	

Friday	

Saturday		Sunday	

Weekly Schedule

Month: _____   **Reminders/Assignments**

Monday	

Tuesday	

Wednesday	

Notes/To Do

Thursday		

Friday		

Saturday		Sunday	

Weekly Schedule

Month: _____   **Reminders/Assignments**

Monday	

Tuesday	

Wednesday	

Notes/To Do

Thursday	

Friday	

Saturday		Sunday	

Weekly Schedule

Month: _____   **Reminders/Assignments**

Monday	

Tuesday	

Wednesday	

Notes/To Do	

Thursday	

Friday	

Saturday	Sunday

Weekly Schedule

Month: _____   **Reminders/Assignments**

Monday	

Tuesday	

Wednesday	

Notes/To Do

Thursday	
Friday	
Saturday	Sunday

Weekly Schedule

Month: _____

Monday	

Tuesday	

Wednesday	

Notes/To Do	

Thursday	

Friday	

Saturday		Sunday	

Weekly Schedule

Month: _____   **Reminders/Assignments**

Monday	

Tuesday	

Wednesday	

Notes/To Do

Thursday			

Friday			

Saturday		Sunday	

Weekly Schedule

Month: _____   **Reminders/Assignments**

Monday	

Tuesday	

Wednesday	

Notes/To Do	

Thursday		

Friday		

Saturday		Sunday	

Weekly Schedule

Month: _____

Reminders/Assignments

Monday	

Tuesday	

Wednesday	

Notes/To Do	

Thursday	

Friday	

Saturday		Sunday	

Weekly Schedule

Month: _____   **Reminders/Assignments**

Monday	

Tuesday	

Wednesday	

Notes/To Do

Thursday	

Friday	

Saturday	Sunday

Weekly Schedule

Month: _____

Reminders/Assignments

Monday	

Tuesday	

Wednesday	

Notes/To Do

Thursday		

Friday		

Saturday		Sunday	

Weekly Schedule

Month: _____   Reminders/Assignments

Monday	

Tuesday	

Wednesday	

Notes/To Do	

Thursday	

Friday	

Saturday		Sunday	

Weekly Schedule

Month: _____

Reminders/Assignments

Monday	

Tuesday	

Wednesday	

Notes/To Do

Thursday	

Friday	

Saturday		Sunday	

Weekly Schedule

Month: _____   **Reminders/Assignments**

Monday	

Tuesday	

Wednesday	

Notes/To Do

Thursday	

Friday	

Saturday	Sunday

Weekly Schedule

Month: _____

Reminders/Assignments

Monday	

Tuesday	

Wednesday	

Notes/To Do

Thursday	

Friday	

Saturday	Sunday

Weekly Schedule

Month: _____   **Reminders/Assignments**

Monday	

Tuesday	

Wednesday	

Notes/To Do

Thursday	

Friday	

Saturday	Sunday

Weekly Schedule

Month: _____   Reminders/Assignments

Monday	

Tuesday	

Wednesday	

Notes/To Do	

Thursday	

Friday	

Saturday		Sunday	

Weekly Schedule

Month: _____   **Reminders/Assignments**

Monday	

Tuesday	

Wednesday	

Notes/To Do

Thursday	

Friday	

Saturday	Sunday

Weekly Schedule

Month: _____   Reminders/Assignments

Monday	

Tuesday	

Wednesday	

Notes/To Do	

Thursday	

Friday	

Saturday		Sunday	

Weekly Schedule

Month: _____

Reminders/Assignments

Monday	

Tuesday	

Wednesday	

Notes/To Do

Thursday

Friday

Saturday

Sunday

Weekly Schedule

Month: _____   **Reminders/Assignments**

Monday	

Tuesday	

Wednesday	

Notes/To Do

Thursday	

Friday	

Saturday		Sunday	

Listen Up!

Tips for sharpening your listening and note-taking skills in class:

✓ Reread previous notes before attending the next lecture.

✓ Pay attention to the speaker's gestures, tone of voice, and body language.

✓ Reread your notes after you've taken them to see if they make sense.

✓ Use abbreviations instead of writing out long or frequently used words.

✓ Stay alert and focused.

✓ Record only what is important.

✓ Read relevant assignments before attending lectures.

✓ Take careful notes on material that is boring, technical, or complicated.

✓ Follow the organization of the lecture in your notes.

✓ Edit your notes after each class while the lecture is still fresh in your memory.

Procrastination 101

Warning!!!

If you find yourself performing any of the following activities, you may have sunk into the depths of classic procrastination. Time's a-wasting, so stop immediately and get back to that research paper!

✓ Checking (and re-checking) your email.

✓ Making several trips to the campus post office to see if random junk mail has been placed in your mailbox.

✓ Satisfying an urgent need to reorganize your CD collection in alphabetical order by musical category.

✓ Calling your parents "just to say hi," and you can honestly say you don't need anything.

✓ Organizing and reorganizing your computer desktop.

✓ Searching the Web for the ultimate screen-saver and wallpaper to download.

✓ Looking for new bargains on the Internet.

✓ Calling your friends on campus to see what's up (even if you just saw them at lunch).

✓ Trying to remember all the lyrics to theme songs from favorite sitcoms of the past and present.

✓ Watching the Weather Channel to find out the weekend forecast for Nepal.

✓ Dusting.

✓ Designing Impressionist sculpture out of pizza boxes, beer cans, or whatever random art supplies you have on hand.

✓ Feeling a sudden urge to watch the entire *Star Wars* trilogy or all of the *Rocky* movies in one sitting.

✓ Taking a trip to Wal-Mart to stock up on toothpaste, soap, shampoo, etc., just in case there is a global shortage of bathroom supplies in the near future.

✓ Doing laundry even though you just did it three days ago.

✓ Going underwear shopping so you can put off doing laundry for a few more days.

✓ Sending your friends a play-by-play email of what you are supposed to be doing right now.

Conversion Tables

LINEAR MEASURE

To Convert	To	Multiply By
centimeters	kilometers	0.00001
centimeters	meters	0.01
centimeters	millimeters	10.0
centimeters	feet	0.0328084
centimeters	inches	0.3937
fathoms	feet	6.0
feet	centimeters	30.48
feet	meters	0.3048
feet	miles, statute	0.0001894
inches	centimeters	2.54
inches	millimeters	25.4
inches	miles, statute	0.00001578
kilometers	feet	3,280.84
kilometers	meters	1,000.0
kilometers	miles, naut.	0.54
kilometers	miles, statute	0.6214
light years	miles, statute	5.878 trillion
meters	centimeters	100.0
meters	feet	3.28084
meters	kilometers	0.001
meters	miles, statute	0.0006214
meters	millimeters	1,000.0
meters	yards	1.093613
microns	meters	0.000001
miles, statute	feet	5,280
miles, statute	kilometers	1.609
miles, statute	miles, naut.	0.8684
millimeters	inches	0.03937
yards	meters	0.9144
yards	miles, statute	0.0005682

AREA

To Convert	To	Multiply By
acres	hectares	0.4047
acres	square fee	43,560.0
acres	sq. miles	0.001562
centares	sq. meters	1.0
hectares	acres	2.471
hectares	sq. miles	0.003861
square cm.	sq. inches	0.155
square feet	sq. inches	144.0
square feet	sq. meters	0.092903
sq. feet	sq. yards	0.111111
sq. inches	sq. cm.	6.4516
sq. meters	sq. yards	1.196
sq. yards	sq. feet	9.0

TEMPERATURE

To Convert	To	Multiply By
Fahrenheit	Celsius	(°F − 32) ÷ 1.8
Celsius	Fahrenheit	(°C × 1.8) + 32

WEIGHT

To Convert	To	Multiply By
grams	kilograms	0.001
grams	ozs., avdp.	0.03527
grams	lbs., avdp.	0.002205
kilograms	lbs., avdp.	2.205
kilograms	ozs., avdp.	35.274
lbs., avdp.	kilograms	0.4536
lbs., avdp.	ozs., avdp.	16.0
lbs., avdp.	ozs., troy	14.5833
lbs., avdp.	lbs., troy	1.21528
ozs., avdp.	grams	28.34952
ozs., avdp.	lbs., avdp.	0.0625
ozs., troy	ozs., avdp.	1.09714
pounds	kilograms	0.4536
tons, long	kilograms	1,016.0
tons, metric	tons, short	1.1023
tons, short	kilograms	907.1848
tons, long	pounds	2,240
tons, short	pounds	2,000
tons, long	tons, short	1.120
tons, short	tons, long	0.89286

VOLUME AND LIQUID

To Convert	To	Multiply By
bushels	cubic inches	2,150.4
cubic cm.	cubic inches	0.06102
cubic cm.	pints, U.S.	0.002113
cubic feet	cubic meters	0.02832
cubic inches	cubic cm.	16.3871
gallons, U.S.	liters	3.785
liters	cubic cm.	1,000.0
liters	cubic inches	61.024
liters	gal., U.S.	0.2642
liters	milliliters	1,000.0
liters	pints, U.S.	2.113
milliliters	liters	0.001
pints, U.S.	cubic cm.	473.2
pints, U.S.	cubic inches	28.875
pints, U.S.	gal., U.S.	0.125
pints, U.S.	quarts, U.S.	0.5
quarts, dry	cubic inches	67.20
quarts, liq.	cubic inches	57.75
quarts, liq.	gal., U.S.	0.25
quarts, liq.	liters	0.9463

SPEED

To Convert	To	Multiply By
feet/min.	cm./sec.	0.5080
feet/sec.	miles/hr.	0.6818
km./hr	knots	0.5396
knots	feet/hr.	6,076.1
knots	statute mi./hr.	1.151

Useful Information

Commonly Mispelled Words

accept (cf. except)	definite	height	noticeable	remuneration
accidentally	dependent	hindrance	nuisance	resemblance
accommodate	design			reverence
acquaintance	devise (cf. device)	incredible	occasion	ridiculous
acquire	diminution	independent	occurred	
address	disappearance	irresistible	occurrence	seize
all right (cf. alright)	dispel	its (cf. it's)	offered	separate
already (cf. all ready)			omitted	similar
argument	effect (cf. affect)	judgment		special
arithmetic	embarrass		parallel	stationary
athletics	environment	library	peculiar	(immobile)
attendance	exaggerate	literature	possess	stationery
	existence	lose (cf. loose)	preceding	(paper)
beginning			(cf. proceeding)	succeed
believe	familiar	maintenance	prejudice	
benign	fascinate	(cf. maintain)	principal	than (cf. then)
business	flagrant	mathematics	(cf. principle)	their (cf. there, they're)
	foreign	minuscule	privilege	threshold
cemetery	forth (cf. fourth)	miracle		too
changeable	fulfill or fulfil	miscellaneous	quite (cf. quiet)	(cf. to, two)
chief		mischief		tragedy
choose (cf. chose)	government		receive	truly
conscious		necessary	referring	
correspondent	harass	neighbor	relieve	usually

whose (cf. who's)
withhold

Commonly Confused Words

accept, except. *Accept* means "to take or receive"; *except* means "excluding."

affect, effect. The verb *affect* means "to influence." *Effect* as a noun means "a result" and, rarely, as a verb means "to cause something to happen."

as, like. Used as a preposition, *as* indicates a precise comparision. *Like* indicates a resemblance or similiarity.

bad, badly. Use *bad* (adjective) with a noun or linking verb expressing feelings, not the adverb *badly*.

complement, compliment. *Complement* means "an accompaniment"; *compliment* means "words of praise."

farther, further. *Farther* implies a distance that can be measured; *further* implies one that cannot.

fewer, less. Use *fewer* for things that can be counted, and use *less* for quantities that cannot be divided.

good, well. *Good* (an adjective) means "favorable" (a good trip). *Well* (an adverb) means "done favorably." Avoid informal uses of *good* for *well*.

lay, lie. Use *lay* to place an object and *lie* to position the self.

principal, principle. *Principal* is a noun meaning "an authority" or "head of a school" or an adjective meaning "leading." *Principle* is a noun meaning "belief or conviction."

than, then. *Than* is use to compare; *then* implies a sequence of events.

who, whom. Though the distinction between these words is disappearing, many expect the formal *whom* for an object.

Useful Information

U.S. POSTAL ABBREVIATIONS

AL	Alabama	KS	Kansas	ND	North Dakota
AK	Alaska	KY	Kentucky	OH	Ohio
AS	American Samoa	LA	Louisiana	OK	Oklahoma
AZ	Arizona	ME	Maine	OR	Oregon
AR	Arkansas	MD	Maryland	PA	Pennsylvania
CA	California	MA	Massachusetts	PR	Puerto Rico
CO	Colorado	MI	Michigan	RI	Rhode Island
CT	Connecticut	MN	Minnesota	SC	South Carolina
DE	Delaware	MS	Mississippi	SD	South Dakota
DC	District of Columbia	MO	Missouri	TN	Tennessee
FL	Florida	MT	Montana	TX	Texas
GA	Georgia	NE	Nebraska	UT	Utah
GU	Guam	NV	Nevada	VT	Vermont
HI	Hawaii	NH	New Hampshire	VA	Virginia
ID	Idaho	NJ	New Jersey	WA	Washington
IL	Illinois	NM	New Mexico	WV	West Virginia
IN	Indiana	NY	New York	WI	Wisconsin
IA	Iowa	NC	North Carolina	WY	Wyoming

U.S. UNITS OF MEASURE

Length
1 foot = 12 inches
1 yard = 3 feet
1 mile = 1,760 yards

Volume
1 pint = 16 fl. ounces
1 quart = 2 pints
1 gallon = 4 quarts

Weight
1 ounce = 16 grams
1 pound = 16 ounces
1 ton = 2,000 pounds

MATH SYMBOLS

π	pi	f	function	$\cap$	intersection
Σ	sum (sigma)	$\sqrt{}$	square root	$\circ$	infinity
Δ	difference (delta)	$\emptyset$	null set	$\uparrow$	not equal
$\char`\^$	exponent	$\cup$	union	$\oplus$	approximately equal

SCIENTIFIC UNITS OF MEASURE

Unit or Constant	Abbreviation	Measures
ampere	amp	electric current
astronomical unit	AU	astronomical distance
calorie	cal	energy
hertz	Hz	frequency
joule	J	energy
kelvin	K	heat
ohm	Ω	electrical resistance
volt	V	electromotive force
watt	W	power

lxxxiv

Web Resources

Google
The world's largest search engine for information seekers of all types
http://www.google.com

AltaVista: Babel Fish
The first Internet machine translation service that can translate words, phrases or entire Web sites to and from English, Spanish, French, German, Portuguese, Italian, and Russian
http://world.altavista.com

Merriam-Webster OnLine
A dictionary and thesaurus based on the print version of *Merriam-Webster's Collegiate® Dictionary, Tenth Edition*
http://www.m-w.com

Encyclopedia.com
An encyclopedia and eLibrary digital archive with more than 57,000 frequently updated articles from the *Columbia Encyclopedia, Sixth Edition*; includes links to newspaper and magazine articles, as well as pictures and maps
http://www.encyclopedia.com

MyWritingLab and **MyReadingLab**
Comprehensive practice on the major skills and writing topics at MyWritingLab, and at MyReadingLab are practice formats for sharpening reading skills
http://www.mywritinglab.com and *www.myreadinglab.com*

MySkillsLab
A practice site for reading and writing skills
http://www.myskillslab.com

Bartleby.com
A comprehensive literary archive and online reference publisher of nonfiction works
http://www.bartleby.com

The Weather Channel
Features current conditions and forecasts for over 77,000 locations worldwide, along with weather-related news, educational material, a weather glossary, a storm encyclopedia, and seasonal features
http://www.weather.com

America Online's CityGuide
A wide variety of information about things to do, buy, and see in your town—local entertainment, commerce, news, and community resources for residents and visitors in 319 cities across the country
http://cityguide.aol.com

CNN.com
Online news and information delivery updated 24/7 by 4,000 news professionals; features the latest multimedia technologies, from live video streaming to searchable archives
http://www.cnn.com

Slate.com
An online magazine with informed perspectives on news, politics, and culture
http://www.slate.com

PBS
A non-profit media enterprise operated by the nation's 349 public television stations; delve further into the subjects you most enjoy—from news to history and the arts to science and technology
http://www.pbs.org

NPR
A not-for-profit producer and distributor of noncommercial news, talk, and entertainment programming; more than 290 hours of original programming each week
http://www.npr.org

United States Postal Service
Find mailing information, buy stamps, pay bills, and more
http://www.usps.com

MapQuest
Online mapping and driving directions—print, download, or email personalized maps; access millions of locations around the world and find businesses
http://www.mapquest.com

Personal Links

_____

_____

_____

_____

_____

Name	Home
Address	Office
	Cell
	Email

Name	Home
Address	Office
	Cell
	Email

Name	Home
Address	Office
	Cell
	Email

Name	Home
Address	Office
	Cell
	Email

Name	Home
Address	Office
	Cell
	Email

Name	Home
Address	Office
	Cell
	Email

Contact Information

Name	Home
Address	Office
	Cell
	Email

Name	Home
Address	Office
	Cell
	Email

Name	Home
Address	Office
	Cell
	Email

Name	Home
Address	Office
	Cell
	Email

Name	Home
Address	Office
	Cell
	Email

Name	Home
Address	Office
	Cell
	Email

Name	Home
Address	Office
	Cell
	Email

Name	Home
Address	Office
	Cell
	Email

Name	Home
Address	Office
	Cell
	Email

Name	Home
Address	Office
	Cell
	Email

Name	Home
Address	Office
	Cell
	Email

Name	Home
Address	Office
	Cell
	Email

Contact Information

Name	Home
Address	Office
	Cell
	Email

Name	Home
Address	Office
	Cell
	Email

Name	Home
Address	Office
	Cell
	Email

Name	Home
Address	Office
	Cell
	Email

Name	Home
Address	Office
	Cell
	Email

Name	Home
Address	Office
	Cell
	Email

Contact Information

Name	Home
Address	Office
	Cell
	Email

Name	Home
Address	Office
	Cell
	Email

Name	Home
Address	Office
	Cell
	Email

Name	Home
Address	Office
	Cell
	Email

Name	Home
Address	Office
	Cell
	Email

Name	Home
Address	Office
	Cell
	Email

Contact Information

Name	Home
Address	Office
	Cell
	Email

Name	Home
Address	Office
	Cell
	Email

Name	Home
Address	Office
	Cell
	Email

Name	Home
Address	Office
	Cell
	Email

Name	Home
Address	Office
	Cell
	Email

Name	Home
Address	Office
	Cell
	Email

Contact Information

Name	Home
Address	Office
	Cell
	Email

Name	Home
Address	Office
	Cell
	Emial

Name	Home
Address	Office
	Cell
	Email

Name	Home
Address	Office
	Cell
	Email

Name	Home
Address	Office
	Cell
	Email

Name	Home
Address	Office
	Cell
	Email

Name	Home
Address	Office
	Cell
	Email

Name	Home
Address	Office
	Cell
	Email

Name	Home
Address	Office
	Cell
	Email

Name	Home
Address	Office
	Cell
	Email

Name	Home
Address	Office
	Cell
	Email

Name	Home
Address	Office
	Cell
	Email

Name		Home
Address		Office
		Cell
		Email

Name		Home
Address		Office
		Cell
		Email

Name		Home
Address		Office
		Cell
		Email

Name		Home
Address		Office
		Cell
		Email

Name		Home
Address		Office
		Cell
		Email

Name		Home
Address		Office
		Cell
		Email

Contact Information

Name	Home
Address	Office
	Cell
	Email

Name	Home
Address	Office
	Cell
	Email

Name	Home
Address	Office
	Cell
	Email

Name	Home
Address	Office
	Cell
	Email

Name	Home
Address	Office
	Cell
	Email

Name	Home
Address	Office
	Cell
	Email

Contact Information

Name		Home
Address		Office
		Cell
		Email

Name		Home
Address		Office
		Cell
		Email

Name		Home
Address		Office
		Cell
		Email

Name		Home
Address		Office
		Cell
		Email

Name		Home
Address		Office
		Cell
		Email

Name		Home
Address		Office
		Cell
		Email

Contact Information

Name	Home
Address	Office
	Cell
	Email

Name	Home
Address	Office
	Cell
	Email

Name	Home
Address	Office
	Cell
	Email

Name	Home
Address	Office
	Cell
	Email

Name	Home
Address	Office
	Cell
	Email

Name	Home
Address	Office
	Cell
	Email

Contact Information

Name	Home
Address	Office
	Cell
	Email

Name	Home
Address	Office
	Cell
	Email

Name	Home
Address	Office
	Cell
	Email

Name	Home
Address	Office
	Cell
	Email

Name	Home
Address	Office
	Cell
	Email

Name	Home
Address	Office
	Cell
	Email

Notes

Notes

Notes

Notes

Notes

Notes

Notes

Notes

Notes

Notes